D1724098

The Relationship Between 'I' And 'Me'

Between Absolute Splendour and Captive Splendour

Ramesh S. Balsekar

Books by Ramesh S. Balsekar

- Let Life Flow (2005)
- Seeking Enlightenment — Why ? (2005)
- Nuggets of Wisdom (2005)
- The One in the Mirror (2004)
- The Wisdom of Balsekar (2004)
- The Seeking (2004)
- Confusion No More (2003)
- Guru Pournima (2003)
- Peace and Harmony in Daily Living (2003)
- The Ultimate Understanding (2001)
- Advaita, the Buddha and the Unbroken Whole (2000)
- It So Happened That... The Unique Teaching of Ramesh S. Balsekar (2000)
- Sin and Guilt: Monstrosity of Mind (2000)
- Meaningful Trivialities from the Source (2000)
- The Infamous Ego (1999)
- Who Cares?! (1999)
- The Essence of the Bhagavad Gita (1999)
- Your Head in the Tiger's Mouth (1997)
- Consciousness Writes (1996)
- Consciousness Speaks (1996)
- A Net of Jewels (1996)
- The Bhagavad Gita – A Selection (1995)
- Ripples (1994)

ॐ

प्रातः स्मरामि हृदि संस्फुरदात्मतत्त्वं
सच्चित्सुखं परमहंसगतिं तुरीयम् ।
यत् स्वप्नजागरसुषुप्तमवैति नित्यं
तदब्रह्म निष्कलमहं न च भूतसंघः ॥

———— ∾ ————

In the early morning meditation,
I concentrate on that Primal Energy
—throbbing in the centre of my Heart,
That Impersonal Awareness —I Am —
which transcends the three states of
dreaming-waking-deep sleep,
That Pure Source —Brahman —
which I am in Reality,
and not this psychosomatic apparatus.

- Shankaracharya's *Atma-bodha*

The Relationship Between 'I' And 'Me'

Between Absolute Splendour and Captive Splendour

Ramesh S. Balsekar

Edited by Chaitan S. Balsekar

Copyright © 2006 by Ramesh S. Balsekar
First Edition May 2006

Published by
ZEN PUBLICATIONS
43/D6 Nivera Society, SVP Nagar, Mhada, Four Bungalows,
Andheri (West), Mumbai 400 053. India. Tel: (+91 22) 3240 8074
eMail: zenpublications@gmail.com
Website: www.zenpublications.com

ISBN-81-88071-26-9

All rights reserved. No part of this book may be reproduced or transmitted in any
form or by any means, electronic or mechanical, including photocopying, recording,
or by any information storage and retrieval system without written permission from
the author or his agents, except for the inclusion of brief quotations in a review.

The Relationship Between 'I' And 'Me'

―――――――――――― ∾ ――――――――――――

Who am I?

Who is this me that lives as a doer of his deeds?
This is the basic, the only sadhana, Raman Maharshi suggested to
the seekers.

Basically, in daily living, the "me" can only mean that which is
always seeking, in every situation, the " correct" answer to the
question and the "right" action in the circumstances — both based
on his desires and his wants. But he has never had any control
over what actually happens in any situation. Therefore, he is
constantly buffeted between pleasure and pain.

The "me" is the very basis of the mechanism of daily living. In any
situation, the "me" has to decide what he will do in order to get
what he wants — total free will.

Intrinsically, the "me" can only be the impersonal consciousness
identified with the body-mind organism as identified consciousness:
a separate entity with autonomy and personal doership, commonly
referred to as the "ego".

It is this "me", the ego,that investigates itself and asks:"Who am I?"

All along he was thinking he was a human being, a person or an individual with a name, different and separate from other individuals and objects in the world, a thinker of his thoughts, experiencer of his emotions and feelings, with intellect and free will to take decisions and act on those decisions, with family, friends and others, holding a position in life, having certain assets, and so on.

Now he is asking himself: "Am I really all this or am I something more ?"

Am I this name that I have? No. It is something to identify me with, and it can always be changed.

Am I this human being? I think I am a human being because I am identifying myself with this human body. I am that which is aware of this body and not this body itself. Of course, my presence here is because of this body and because of the life in this body. If this body dies, where am I? Where was I before this body was born? However, the fact remains that I am not this human body but that which is aware of this body, and right now, which is limited by this body.

Am I these thoughts? No. I am that which is aware of these thoughts. They rise and set in me, but I remain.

Am I these emotions and feelings? No. I am that which is aware of them as they rise and set in me. As an ego, I identify myself with them, but I am not them. They rise and set in me but I remain.

Am I this intellect and free will? As an ego, I think I own them and use them. Really speaking, I am only aware of them as they are being used in the day-to-day living of this ego that I think I am.

Finally, am I this ego, this person, this individual that I think I am, separate from other individuals and objects? No, I am really that which is aware of this ego in its day-to-day living as a human being, as Mr. XYZ, thinking he is a thinker of his thoughts, experiencer of his emotions and feelings, and the doer of his acts with intellect and free will.

Who or what am I really? Obviously, I am that Pure Impersonal Awareness which is aware of all this, that which is prior to thought, that in which thoughts rise and set. I am that Presence of which the ego is always aware even before it thinks of itself as a person or individual. If that be so, then what is the connection between this Impersonal Awareness or Consciousness or Presence and this human being and this ego and all the accompanying baggage?

Before the body was born or came into existence in the manifestation which is the dream of Consciousness, I was Pure, Impersonal Consciousness or Awareness. When the body was born, this Impersonal Consciousness or Awareness got reflected in this body as the reflected I AM or Presence. This reflected I AM got identified with this body, and a body/mind organism got created which became this human being with this ego and its intellect and free will, its sense of doership and separateness.

With this enquiry, I, the ego come to the following Understanding: That which I think I am is a human being with its ego and the accompanying baggage.

That which I think I am i.e. this human being with its independence and free will is actually nothing but a role, an instrument or a robot.

That which I am is Pure, Impersonal Consciousness which is now this Identified Consciousness reflecting in this body and which is now playing this ego role.

Now I am intellectually aware that I am this Pure Impersonal Awareness, but so long as life is there in the body, I continue to be a human being with its intellect and free will and doership. Therefore, I continue to live as a human being using my intellect and free will and my sense of doership. But now there is a difference. All along I thought I was the Actor, but now I have realized, intellectually though it may be, that I am a Role played by the Divine Actor, nothing but an instrument, a robot.

I continue to live as a human being, as an Ego or a person, as a "me" centre, thinking, deciding, desiring, acting, suffering, enjoying, but all along with the understanding that no matter what I may think or feel or do or want, I am actually being lived.

Externally, the ego is essentially influenced in his daily living by two Factors: genes and conditioning. Basically of course, the genes constitute a very powerful factor, and as more and more research throws out, almost everything that happens to the body-mind organism and through the body-mind organism can be traced to the genes. But the general attitude of the ego towards life and living is based on conditioning and the beliefs the conditioning generates— conditioning at home, conditioning in the relevant society, conditioning in the school in that society, conditioning according to religion.

The "me", the ego-centre, is necessarily a mass of conditioning —bound to the family, to the property, to the community, to the society, to the culture. The basic problem in life is to have this ego-centre and yet live fully in the world ; live in harmony with the other and in peace with oneself. Is it possible to live in this world understanding the ego-centre and doing your job, doing everything with vitality, without the burden of the ego-centre ? Of course, one does need the experience of the past to use in the present moment.

What this means is that the working mind must have the total control over the problem and the solution, depending upon the experience of the past, without being burdened by the conditioning of seeing everything fragmentarily, so that we are capable of being sensitive to the whole.

The problem, in other words is: how to do something so that the ego-centre scores over the "other", but the fact remains that whatever one does in a given situation, what actually happens — and the consequences of that happening—has never been in our control. In daily living, therefore, for this very reason it is totally futile to blame anyone for any ultimate happening.

Not to blame anyone means freedom from guilt and shame for one's own actions, and freedom from hatred for the "other" for his actions: peace for oneself and harmony with the other.

❧

The Impersonal Consciousness and the Ego

ꝏ

Among spiritual seekers, it is an accepted fact that the Ego is basically, fundamentally, the Impersonal Consciousness identified with a particular body-mind organism, and a name as a separate entity, with a sense of personal doership which establishes a relationship with the "other" separate entity. And it is this interhuman relationship that is the basis of the functioning of manifestation, which we know as life.

What has caused considerable discussion is where exactly is this identification in the body/mind organism located? British neurologist and Nobel-Laureate John Eccles considered Impersonal Consciousness to be extra-cerebral, and specified an area in the brain where fusion of consciousness with brain takes place. This region is called supplementary motor area, SMA—located at the top of the physical brain. He also held that by a complex code, the extra-cerebral mind plays 50 million neurons in the SMA region. Eccles believes that the non-physical mind survives after the death of the physical body and brain.

This concept fits in perfectly with the spiritual concept that it is the Source— the Impersonal Consciousness —which identifies itself with each body/mind organism and creates the separate entity with the sense of personal doership. When the body dies, the Consciousness identified with a particular body/mind organism, gets freed from the bondage of the organism and becomes intermingled with the Impersonal Consciousness.

Bell's Theorem has also proved infinite inter-connectedness of each part of the Universe which throws light on the phenomenon of Consciousness. If the Universe is inter-connected in an infinite and immediate way, it obviously means that every human brainwork can inter-penetrate every other brainwork, and this establishes that there is only one Cosmic brain or Cosmic Consciousness, the Source itself.

It can therefore be considered validly that the Impersonal or Cosmic Consciousness is the software operator behind the hardware of the entire physical brain complex. In other words, Cosmic Consciousness is an actual phenomenon at whose dictates the brain works. It is obviously beyond our body, but functions through the body/mind organism and controls both its voluntary and involuntary functions.

Psychologist Jung held that personal consciousness of the individual is connected with Collective Consciousness, the Universal Consciousness. As Schrodinger has put it: "Consciousness is always in the singular; the plurality of Consciousness is Maya."

It is the separate entity—the identified consciousness—which has to live his or her life and seek peace and harmony in daily living. For this reason, the identified consciousness as the ego-centre must clearly understand its relationship with the impersonal consciousness.

Consciousness must necessarily be present in the body-mind organism every split second of the day; this it does either in its impersonal state in deep sleep or under sedation or in the Samadhi state, or in its identified state as the ego-centre in the waking state and the dreaming state. The basic seeking in daily living is the ego-centre seeking in the waking state that deep peace that exists in deep sleep. For this reason it is absolutely necessary for the ego-centre to seek earnestly and find out what at present prevents that peace from happening in daily living.

The space or interval between two thoughts is the Impersonal Consciousnes or Awareness, the I AM which has identified with body to create the body/mind organism. Thoughts rise and set in the body/mind organism to create the ego-centre. The ego-centre creates a space around itself, and that space is necessarily limited. This is the space of isolation with one's ambition, one's frustrations, one's anger, one's sensuality, one's growth, one's meditation, one's wanting to reach nirvana. One's relationship with the other—the basis of daily living—is the image of that isolation. The question, therefore, is : is it possible for the ego-centre not to create space around itself, build a wall around itself, isolation, a prison and call that "space"?

The basis of the ego-centre in daily living is the relationship between "me" and the "other". The ego-centre is the doer—doing the observing, doing the thinking, doing the experiencing. This is where the battle begins between the observer and the observed. The ego-centre says "this must be changed, not that; this is narrow that is too wide; he is better than I am". All this is the movement in the space between the observer and the observed—the "me' and the "other". When I observe my wife, it is with the image that I have of her: there is always this division and space.

Can the mind empty itself of images? The answer is yes. If I do not form an image NOW, the past images have no place. What actually happens is that if I form an image now, I relate it to past images. By not forming an image now, the mind gets emptied of all earlier images. And in that emptiness, space disappears and something incredibly beautiful happens — a sense of deep peace in the absence of images.

It is not what is out there but what I see out there that is relevant. "Two men looked out from behind prison walls. One saw the bars while the other saw the stars." I can see you as a personality out there, but I can also see you as Consciousness appearing as you. I can relate with you as a person, an image, but at the same time I can also relate with you as Consciousness appearing as you. I can see myself as an ego, a person, an image relating with you, another person, another ego, another image. At the same time, I can also see both myself and you free from images — as Consciousness relating to Consciousness, Consciousness relating to itself in the game of life. Consciousness is all there is.

The creation of images is due to the sense of personal doership, which disappears with the total acceptance that observing happens without any individual doer of observing; similarly, thinking, doing, experiencing HAPPENS without any individual doer.

There is the tradition of the weavers in India and other places. They can weave without a pattern and yet they weave in a tradition which is so deeply rooted that they do not have to think about it. It comes out spontaneously through their hands. Also there is the tradition of the scientist, the biologist, the anthropologist, which is tradition in the form of accumulation of knowledge, handed over by one scientist to another scientist, by a doctor to another doctor,

learning. Perhaps in such cases, tradition is not the right word —
may be a happening according to the Cosmic Law.

∽

Most of us live a very superficial life, and are content to live such
a life meeting our problems superficially and thereby increasing
them. This is because our problems are complex and also subtle
and need deep penetration and understanding. There is a living at
a totally different dimension if we are able to understand ourselves
by penetrating deeper into the levels of our being.

Is it possible to look at oneself totally, to observe the whole
movement of the "me", the ego-centre, with a non-analytical mind
so that there can be instant, total understanding? It is important to
discover whether one can go beyond oneself and find the deeper
reality to live without an illusion, in harmony and in peace. What
this actually means is: is it possible to look without the observer
looking at something observed, without looking through
fragmentation, without any division, both in oneself within and
outwardly, in order to avoid conflict?

What happens now is that when I look at myself, "me" the observer
observes myself according to my culture, according to my
conditioning, and hopes to bring about a change in the observed.
I hope to bring about a change in the "what is" to an illusory
conditioned "what should be" in the illusory future. When I look
at myself, I do that 'in the eyes of the past: past memories, past
delights, past failures, past disappointments—and then judge the
present that is vibrant and moving, not a static thing. Importantly,
analysis is the denial of action.

Therefore, while accepting the "what is", I feel that something is clearly not right, and no amount of analysis is going to put it right. I have two alternatives: (1) I can say to myself that the problem is too big, and I do nothing; or (2) I take immediate action, doing whatever I can do, and let whatever happens, happen according to the Cosmic Law. I prefer to do the latter, and thus live in the present moment.

One may wonder, what is the point of all this. The point is that then the mind is free from any conditioning, without any conflict, totally quiet and peaceful; and it is this very quality of mind that enables it to observe the present without the eyes of the past —a fresh, vibrant present.

∽

A common problem the ego-centre faces in daily living is conflict with the other. The usual conflict is between the husband and the wife. She is attached, dependent upon him emotionally, psychologically, physically and economically. She depends upon him totally. And then one morning he tells her that he likes someone else. Similarly, when you turn against me I am lost because I depend upon you for companionship and for so many other things. So one has to find out why one is so inwardly dependent.

I am lonely, I am frightened deep down and I am incapable of resolving this awful feeling of loneliness. Not knowing how to resolve it, I begin to attach myself to people, to ideas, to groups, to activities, to demonstrations and the rest of it. The problem is how to go beyond this loneliness which man has tried to fight at all times. He feels lonely, empty. incomplete, insufficient, and he projects an outside entity like a Guru representing God. This is the problem of loneliness.

The real question is: can there be a meaningful relationship between two human beings if each one is basically occupied with himself, if each one is really concerned only with his own ambitions and worries and all the absurdity that human beings go through?

One observes how very vital relationship is in life and how very few human beings have broken down the barriers that exist between themselves and the "other". If I have a relationship with another — and daily living from morning to night is based on relationship whether the other is a close relative or a total stranger — it is obvious that the relationship is based on the image I have formed about the "other". A stranger has cheated me and I have formed an image of the "other" as someone to be wary of.

In other words, it is a matter of fact that the relationship is usually based not between two persons but between two images based on what each has been doing. If we observe in our own minds the activity in the relationship, one can see the truth and validity of this fact. Our relationships, are based on what each has been "doing". And the fact of the matter is that there is considerable difference between "doing" and the happening of the consequence of that "doing"

How often have each of us not wondered: "How could I have done such a stupidly vicious deed? I certainly did not mean to do that". The fact of the matter is that in actuality, every "deed" turns out to be a happening based on something over which one has no control. If I analysed any action of "mine", I would find that it was, for instance, the result of a thought that I had. But if that thought had not happened, my action would not have happened, and I had no control over the happening of that thought; indeed no one – not even a sage – has any control over the next thought that would come into his mind. If that thought had not happened, "my" action would not have happened.

A similar result would happen if we analyse any number of actions. If I had not been at a certain place at a certain time, and seen something or heard something or smelt something or touched something, then "my" action would not have happened. And I certainly do not have control over being at a certain place, at a certain time, and for something to happen which I saw (or heard). The fact of the matter is that our relationships are based on what we consider as each other's actions. Actually, all actions, through whichever body-mind organism (mine or the other's) they might have happened, turn out on investigation to be "happenings" over which the person concerned certainly did not have any control. Our relationship is based on images and images are based on what are considered as the actions of those persons. The beauty of it is that these so called actions are not anybody's actions but "happenings".

In the words of the Buddha, "events happen, deeds get done, consequences happen but there is no one doing any deed." The society in which we live, must of course, consider all actions as those of the individuals concerned, and judge them according to the prevailing social considerations and legal provisions. And each of us must necessarily accept and honor such decisions. But our social responsibility is totally different from our responsibility to ourselves, on which depends our happiness, our peace of mind.

The society may honor our deeds but if we truly accept our non-doership, then the society's honor will not be accompanied by the slightest sense of pride or arrogance. Equally, society's blame will not result is any guilt or shame as far as we are concerned.

∾

In daily living, when does the "me" come into the picture? It is when the "me" observes something — the observer as the subject and the observed as the object — the "me" promptly compares what is observed based on his past experience, and judges it as "good" or "bad". The question therefore arises: can the mind observe without the division between the observer and the observed, because what exists is only the observed?

The observer can only be the past, be it the past of a few seconds ago, of yesterday, or of many years. In other words, the observer is surely an entity conditioned in a particular culture, the sum total of past experiences. When the observer says "I don't like this, I want to be that", he has projected "that" from his past knowledge, —past memories, past delights, the things that gave one pleasure and displeasure, the failures, the disappointments, the lack of fulfillment. In other words, the present which is living and moving and not a static dead thing "is viewed with the eyes of the past".

Is it possible to observe the present without the past culture and conditioning? Can the eyes observe without the past? I have an image of myself, created and imposed on me by the culture in which I have lived; I also have my own image of myself: what I am now and what I should be. I have an image about you, about my family, about our political leaders and almost every one in life.

The question is: how can you look without an image, without a distortion? Can the mind be without any image in relationships? It is the image that brings about conflict in relationships. If you give it some serious thought, you will find that it is certainly possible to observe without the eyes of time. And when the mind does so observe, then there is really nothing to be "observed, nothing to be judged. And it is the judgment which causes conflict. In life, it is the judgment that says something is good or bad. When there is no judgment, there is only experience. Whatever Life brings to us is experience. Whatever is being done through us and its consequences are also experience. That's it.

The mind that is not constantly comparing and judging, has no conflict; such a mind is totally quiet and peaceful, not violent. It is then that the mind is truly free, something totally new, without any past images that cloud your mind and create conflict.

∿

Depending on the other is what often causes conflict between the "me" and the other. Psychologically, inwardly, we are all dependent on somebody or the other. Outwardly of course, we cannot stand alone because we need the cook, the servant, the postman, and so on. But inwardly, can we not remain by ourselves, not dependent upon anybody?

Most of us realize, when we do have the courage to face it, that we are terribly lonely, isolated human beings, wanting to escape from it all; being frightened, we run away from it through activity, through attachment, through all forms of worldly or religious entertainment. We isolate ourselves by our daily activities, by our attitudes and our way of thinking. Whatever our relationship with anyone, however intimate, the fact remains that our basic attitude is always self centred; and that causes even more isolation, more loneliness, more dependence on what we expect from the flow of life. And the fact remains that no one has any control over what happens from moment to moment.

The question, the basic question, therefore, is: can I live my daily life without any kind of self-concern because self-concern is my major image? The answer is in one way, astonishingly simple : there is no need to want to live without self-concern, for the simple reason that self-concern — doing, in any situation, whatever one wishes to do in order to get what one wants — is the very basis of the mechanism of daily living!

This is so because the basis of daily living — the mechanism — is precisely the same for the modern man today, or the caveman man 5000 years ago, or the human being in the future, no matter where he is. The human being at any time, in any place does in the given situation, precisely what he wishes to do in order to get what he wants in the circumstances — total freewill.

Everyone's experience however, is that what actually happens as a result of one's action according to one's freewill, has never been in any one's control. What has always happened is one of three things (a) One has got what one wanted (b) One has not got what one wanted; or (c) what one has actually got was totally beyond expectation, for better or for worse. Thereafter, the society in which I live has construed what has happened (and not what I did) as "my" action; the society then judged my action as good or bad, and has rewarded or punished me; reward from the society has meant pleasure in the moment, and punishment has meant pain in the moment. And I am forced to accept the verdict of the society — based on social regulations and legal provisions — if I wish to live in the same society.

  This is the total analysis of the daily living: it begins with my total "free will", but what happens thereafter, has always been God's will expressed through the Society's verdict over which we have absolutely no control. In other words, my responsibility to the society is the basis of my daily living.

The basic question of my self-concern still remains. The trouble is that the human being usually does not address the basic question: WHAT DO I FINALLY WANT IN LIFE?

The ordinary man seeks money or fame together with the usual pleasures of life — that is his "self-concern". Most human beings do not get what they are seeking in their lives and die frustrated. Some of the more fortunate ones do manage to get what they have been seeking — money or fame — but, at some point of time, they realize that deep down they still feel incomplete, inadequate, unfulfilled. And then these few human beings have become "spiritual seekers".

The main trouble with the spiritual seekers is that they are satisfied with the aim of all spiritual seeking. They accept "enlightenment" or self-realization" or some label like that as the goal of spiritual seeking. What they do not do is to ask themselves the vital question "What do I expect "enlightenment" to do for me for the rest of my life that I did not have before?" And therefore, most of the spiritual seekers at the end of their search, remain totally frustrated. It is therefore absolutely essential for the spiritual seekers to realize, preferably through their own thinking and questioning that the ultimate goal of enlightenment is not the total annihilation of pain - physical, psychological, financial — because that is not possible in life. Pain and pleasure is an essential element of the basic duality of every conceivable kind, that is the very essence of the manifestation and its functioning that we call "life". Nor will enlightenment necessarily give one special powers like being in two or three places at the same time or ability to walk on water, or healing. It is therefore absolutely essential to realize deeply that all one expects to get out of enlightenment is the simple but magnificent gift of "peace of mind".

Therefore, self-concern is not the real problem of the seeker. Indeed, self-concern is the essence of the free will of each human being. Whatever one does is always a matter of self-concern, whether it is "selfish" or "generous". Why is a man generous? Because, not being generous will make him feel bad; in order to feel good — self-concern — he is forced to be generous.

∽

It is a fact of life that the human being is interested in his own welfare: more progress, more prestige, more power to dominate others. What is wrong about it? One is naturally interested in oneself fundamentally and yet, one thinks that it is wrong for various reasons, ideologically, traditionally and so on.

The point is that if you are seeking satisfaction in helping others, you are still concerned with yourself. Where is the need to bring in any ideological concept? The point is that one really wants satisfaction, whether it is in sex, in freedom, or in helping others, in being a saint, or whatever. And, of course, the ultimate satisfaction is the peculiar idea of self realization, without realizing what it will do for us by way of satisfaction!

One seeks different ways of finding gratification — through food, sex, important position, through various virtues and so on. Why? It is easy to see that when you need food, you feel gratified when you eat, but why move to another level of satisfaction by wanting more and better food to eat? I also want a good position in society, which is gratifying because then I am secure with a big house with a watchman at the gate, and the rest of it. Apart from the money and the comfort it gives, why this craving for position in society?

Strip the Pope of his robes, or the Sanyasi of his ochre clothes and they would be nobody. Is that it? Are we afraid of being nobody? Why this craving? In a chicken yard, there is an order of pecking. So could it be that we have perhaps inherited this wanting to dominate? In the Kumbha Mela procession, we are told that there is an established order in which the various heads of the Maths follow one another. So perhaps this wanting to dominate has been inherited. The saint who seeks a position in the ashram is surely as aggressive as the chicken pecking in the yard!

The politician is aggressive, the big shots in business are aggressive; so are the big shots in religion. Why? Could it be that fear is the cause of that aggression because the society in which we are forced to live is so constructed that a citizen who has a position of respect is treated with great courtesy, whereas a man who has no position is likely to be kicked around? So, is it that we are aggressive because we are frightened of being nobodies? Or, are we frightened because it has become a habit?

An experiment has been made putting thousands of rats in a very small room; and they lost all sense of proportion. May be human beings are aggressive because we do not have enough space around us physically; this may be one of the reasons for aggression. Also, of course, one could be aggressive because one is frightened. One has to face this question of fear; if we can understand fear, we could find out whether there is a possibility of being free from fear. If we could be free from fear, would there be aggressiveness? Is it possible to live without fear? You are afraid of your neighbor, your boss; he might not give you a raise, he might take away your job; you may be afraid of your wife because she dominates, she nags, she bullies. Why is one afraid? Because one yearns for continuity. She dominates you, she bullies you, she has contempt for you. So what takes place? You are afraid of losing her and you get used to this fear. Gradually, you become duller and duller, and you lose all sensitivity. You rarely smile. Similarly, you have gotten used to the rotten society in which you live. You have got used to the Gita, the Upanishads and all similar crutches, but inwardly you are dull. What are you to do? Is that not the question? I have become completely indifferent, even callous because of various reasons—my family, over population , the enormous burden of thousands of years of tradition, the endless rituals, the squalor inside the house and outside and so on.

I see the cause and the effect and I see that it is impossible to live that way. The point is that if I change because it is painful, then I am pursuing pleasure. It is really this pursuit of pleasure which is the cause of my dullness, indifference, callousness. It is this same seeking after pleasure — pleasure in the family, in the Gods, in the Upanishads, the Quoran, the Bible, in the Establishment. The point is that the origin of the movement which has reduced me to this indifference was the wanting of pleasure. If I revolt against this, it will again be the pursuit of pleasure!

If you watch your own daily living, you will surely realize that it is habit, getting used to something day after day leading to a habit, which is the beginning of indifference. It really is an important discovery: when I pursue pleasure, there will also be the root of indifference. Any pleasure, however intense in the beginning, soon becomes a habit and loses its attraction and leads to indifference. Pleasure becomes a habit, and similarly, likes and dislikes become a habit: all one's judgments are based on likes and dislikes. When the mind clearly watches this whole process and movement of seeking pleasure — and you cannot truly "watch" it if you judge anything— the mind becomes independent, much more sensitive, much more "intelligent", much sharper. The result? I very clearly see that in the actual sight of something beautiful — the curve of a tree or a lovely female form, or whatever — there may be a sense of appreciation, even gratification — but never "pleasure". The pleasure arises only when there is egoic involvement in horizontal time, thinking back on the experience. You seek pleasure because you cannot look at anything without an image, without a symbol, without deciding that you like it or do not like it. And that has become a habit.

"Enjoyment" is natural and is really only a biological reaction to something seen, heard, smelt, tasted or touched. The problem arises when the ego-centre reacts to this natural biological reaction of pleasure and wants "more and more". It is this pursuit of pleasure that is the real problem. There is genuine enjoyment, a deep sense of gratification, only when the mind is free from the known, free from memory. You do need memory and experience for the working mind to work efficiently, but you do not need the thinking mind to go back into the past and project something illusory into the future.

∾

What is going on in the world — violence, disasters, hatreds, corruption — also goes on in ourselves. In the me - centre, one is at war with oneself, unhappy, dissatisfied, violent, aggressive, corrupt, lonely, seeking something vague and unknown. We have tried every form of therapy, religious sanctions and their pursuits, a monastic life, a life of sacrifice, suppression, denial, and yet we seem to be unable to free ourselves from the terrible mess inside ourselves. Is there no way to get out of this confusion?

It may seem far fetched but it is a fact of life that our problem is one of "space" Where there is space, there is silence: not the space created by thought, but space that has no frontiers at all, immeasurable space that cannot be conceived by thought. When the human being has space — real space, width and depth not conceived by thought — there can be absolute silence. However, we have no space ecologically, socially or more important, in our own mind. This is perhaps the main reason for the violence.

We do not want be hurt anymore; so we withdraw, we resist, we build a sort of wall around ourselves and those we love and like, and that means a very limited space. And it is from this very small, narrow space that the me-centre functions and acts in relation to the "other". In that chattering mind, crowded with information, rumours, opinion, fears, there is hardly any space at all. And in that restricted space functions the me-centre with its horizontal thinking, conceptualizing, objectivizing. What happens is that, as a result, there is isolation, division, conflict in all kinds of relationships.

The real problem, therefore, for the me-centre is: I want to live a life of delight, pleasure and beauty, and I also want that which is immeasurable, beyond the fancy of thought. I am aware of the movement, the demand, the pursuit of pleasure, with all its fears, travails, sorrow, agony and anxiety. I also know that there is a kind of cool, quiet happiness that is totally uinvited, which thought can never capture. So the problem is that the ego-centre wants to have both — the things both of this world and of the other world.

In this problem, the real question is: does the me-centre with its thinking system see the two sides of this problem, or is there another totally different factor which clearly sees this difference and finally penetrates the problem and cuts off this "Gordian Knot"? Could this different factor be called "intelligence", and if this be so, what is the relationship between "intelligence" and thought or horizontal thinking ? The answer is astonishingly simple: the division lies essentially in the fact that the pleasure and joy that the mind — the ego-centre — seeks is entirely contained in the flow of life. The flow of life means basically pleasure one moment and pain in the next moment. The important fact of life is that the flow of life is beyond the control of any person — the sage or the ordinary person.

Therefore, it is totally futile to seek and desire only pleasure in the flow of life while avoiding the pain.

The other kind of quiet happiness beyond the confines of horizontal thinking and conceptualizing, is contained not in the flow of life but in our attitude to the flow of life. Our attitude to life so far, which has prevented the happening of this special kind of happiness — peace and harmony — is based on the fact that our attitude to life, concerning the relationship with the "other" is antagonistic to the "other". Hundreds of years of conditioning inherited since childhood has made us think of the "other" as a potential rival, potential enemy. This attitude has created a tremendous burden of hatred — hatred towards ourselves because of the guilt and shame for hurting others, and hatred towards others for hurting us — which has made it impossible for peace and harmony to prevail in our lives.

With this clear understanding, it is obvious that for peace and harmony to prevail in our lives, the basis of our relationship with the other must fundamentally change. Our present attitude is clearly based on what the "other" may do to me that could hurt me one way or the other. The only way this attitude can change is to be able to accept TOTALLY the concept that everything in the world is a happening according to the Cosmic Law, that how each happening (which may happen through any body-mind organism) affects whom — for better or for worse — can also be only according to the Cosmic Law; the basis of the Cosmic Law the human brain is incapable of ever knowing because of the vastness and the complexity of the Cosmic Law which concerns the entire Universe for all time. In other words, no one is capable of "doing" anything, and therefore, no one need be blamed for anything.

This is the only way "Universal Brotherhood" can happen : Universal Brotherhood among human instruments; it cannot happen between rivals and potential enemies.

∾

With the total acceptance that everything in the world is a "happening" according to the Cosmic Law, the question does arise: Does it mean then that the human has no free will at all in his daily living? This is a valid question. And the answer is to say the least, intriguing. Most masters have said that personal effort is necessary for the Understanding to happen; and at some other time they have also said that personal effort is an obstruction to the happening of the ultimate understanding.

The answer is, in a way, exceedingly simple, even obvious. The very basis of the mechanism of daily living is that every human being, in any situation, at any time and place- even the caveman 5000 years ago — has to deal with the situation in which he finds himself; and dealing with a situation obviously means (a) deciding what he wants in the situation, and (b) doing whatever he feels he should do. Total effort according to his own freewill. In other words, daily living, as we know it, cannot happen unless every human being does have total free will to do whatever he feels like doing in the situation. However, there is also the understanding that this total free will is subject to the genes and the conditioning (with its consequent beliefs) of each individual. In effect, therefore, daily living means total freewill for the individual human being to do, whatever he wishes in any given situation knowing all the time that whatever he thinks and does is exactly what he is being lived to think and do, and also, thereafter, as has been everyone's experience what happens is according to God's will or according to a Cosmic Law.

This is precisely what is meant in the Bhagavad Gita (1 V–16–18) when Lord Krishna explains to Arjun:

> One who sees work in no work and no work in work,
> is indeed wise and worthy of liberation from Sansar

The process of "Karma" starts as soon as thought enters the mind and translates itself into action in the form of speech or physical action or both. "Karma" can therefore be analysed as being performed by the mind in thought, by the tongue in speech and by the body in action.

The Bhagavad Gita classifies Karma under three categories: Karma, vi-Karma and a-Karma. Karma is the action which is acceptable to the society according to the social regulations and legal provisions and results in pleasure in the moment; Vi-Karma is action not acceptable to the society, and results in punishment i.e. pain in the moment; A-Karma is non-action which leads to peace and harmony because there is neither pride in the "good" action nor guilt in the "bad" action, based on the Understanding that the result of all actions are based on God's Will according to Cosmic Law.

As Lord Krishna says in the Bhagavad Gita (V-8):

"The Sage centred in Brahman has the constant understanding "I am doing nothing". He is totally firm in the thought that all action is a reaction of the senses to their respective objects — eyes seeing, the ears hearing — (according to the genes and conditioning in the body, created by God).

Of course, "non-action" is totally different from inaction, which is negative doing as opposed to positive doing.

The me-centre is always afraid of coming to an end — and that is what death is. Fear prevents the me-centre from living freely and fear prevents him from looking at what death actually means. Fear demands comfort and so there is the idea of re-birth/re-incarnation, and the idea of doing good Karma. The real problem however, is whether the mind can face the reality of an ending. Anything can happen at any time — old age, heart attack, or some other disease, or accident.

Is it possible to accept the matter of death as the ending, knowing that trying to find comfort is an escape from the fact? Ancient and modern civilizations have tried to go beyond that, to somehow conquer it, to imagine there is immortality, a life after death — anything but face it. The question is : can the mind face something of which it knows absolutely nothing? One is full of other people's knowledge, but obviously such knowledge can only be speculation about a matter such as an ending called death. One may not consciously acknowledge it, but it is there in the blood because one has been brought up in this civilization and culture. And death is something of which no one can know anything; all one knows is that one is frightened of coming to an end, and that is what death is.

It is fear that prevents us from looking at death just as fear has prevented us from living without guilt and anxiety. Fear has prevented us from facing life and fear prevents us from facing death, from looking at what death is. Fear breeds choice, will, resistance, and this is a waste of energy. It is only because one has lived a life of resistance, choice and will that there is fear of not being, of not living. To repeat, fear demands comfort and continuity and so there is the concept of re-birth, another life and so on.

Nothing is known about the happening called death, except that there is an organic death: life will go out of the body and the body will be cremated or buried. Is it not possible for the mind to look at the phenomenon called death as something inevitable, and without any fear? The answer is : only if it understands who the ego-centre "me" really is. The "me" is without the slightest doubt, only Consciousness — Impersonal Consciousness which has identified itself with a particular body-mind organism as a separate entity as "identified consciousness" so that life and living can happen through that entity according to Cosmic Law. Therefore, obviously, *all that happens at death is that the identification gets dissolved and Consciousness regains its impersonality.*

We now come back to our original question: Who am I — who or what is this "me" who lives as the "doer" of his/her actions? As said earlier, the only answer is that the "me" can be, only— Consciousness: impersonal consciousness which has identified with each human body as a separate entity, so that life and living can happen through inter-human relationships happening through the various ego-centres. When the living is over — death happens — the identification is over because it is no longer required.

The final question that remains is: with the clear understanding that the "me" is, from one perspective only the body-mind instrument through which life happens according to the Cosmic Law; and from the other perspective, the "me" can be nothing other than the Impersonal Consciousness, identified with each body-mind organism as identified Consciousness functioning through each body-mind organism as a separate entity — how does such an "enlightened" me live his daily life?

In the Bhagvad Gita, there is a detailed description of the STITAPRAGNYA, precisely as an answer to this very question. But one cannot keep wondering if there cannot be a simpler, more straightforward answer. I would venture to give that answer as follows:

With the total understanding that we are all being lived and that everything is a happening according to the Cosmic Law, whichever way it may affect anyone, for better or worse, he lives his daily life without blaming anyone for anything — without judging or condemning anyone — so that he does not carry any burden of hatred for any personal action towards anyone — neither himself nor the "other". Freed from the sense of doership that is the Divine Hypnosis, he realises that we are all nothing but illusory roles played by the Divine Actor who is all there is. He does not feel separate from the Source and transcends the pain of separation.

Since he has to live in society, he accepts whatever the flow of life brings him from moment to moment — sometimes pleasure, sometimes pain — based on the prevailing social regulations and legal provisions. With the total acceptance of the 'What Is', he remains fulfilled at all times.

In other words, he witnesses life as it happens, without judging or condemning anyone — neither himself nor anyone else — without any regrets for the past, without any complaints about the present, without any expectations for the future.

∾

E D I T O R ' S   N O T E

I was happy and grateful for being given this opportunity by my brother, Ramesh, to edit this booklet. It has been a pleasure to do so.

There is nothing new under the sun is the age old saying. What Ramesh has been writing and speaking about is nothing new in the Philosophy of Advaita, but he has certainly made it clearer for the common man to understand it. However, I have always felt that he has also to be given the recognition for being lived to bring out and focus on two important aspects of Advaita and make it applicable to daily living.

The first is the full definition of the Ego in the Advaita Philosophy. Most people understand the Ego as being identification with a name and form. They have forgotten the most crucial and critical aspect of the Ego, viz. the sense of doership of the Ego. It is to Ramesh's credit that he has focused on and hammered away at the full definition of the Ego, viz. the Ego is the identification with a name and form WITH A SENSE OF DOERSHIP. It is the understanding the villainy of this sense of doership that is the essence of the essence of Applied Advaita in daily living.

Most teachers tell us to kill the Ego, and this is the second aspect. Here again, Ramesh has been lived to stress on the important clarification that so long as there is life in the body, the Ego will have to be there. The Ego cannot be killed. No person, whether a saint, a sage or the common man can live without identifying with his body and his name. According to Ramesh, what distinguishes the sage from the common man is the absence of the most critical aspect of the Ego in the sage's Ego, viz. his sense of doership.

It has to be clearly understood that it is this sense of doership of the Ego that keeps the Ego separate from the Source and causes the pain of separation. As Nisargadata Maharaj used to say: "Understanding is all." One can only wait for the Understanding to blossom forth from the Intellectual to the Experiential.

∾

How do I live my life?

I have sometimes been asked how I spend the day. The intention is obvious — the visitors want to know if there is a clear difference between the way I live and the usual way — for instance, the way I react to situations involving pleasure or pain. All I could say was that truly there is no difference from anyone else. So I thought I would analyze my day and write down how I live my life on a normal day.

1. I sometimes look out on the road and see something happening — a car being parked, and there is a realization that a spontaneous reaction happens: A job well done or badly done. There is a very clear realization that the reaction is a purely spontaneous one in the body-mind organism according to the programming and not 'my' reaction. A similar thing happens in the case of something seen on the television program, e.g. an advertisement well done or badly done: a reaction in the body-mind organism and not 'my' reaction.

2. Whenever there are a few moments (between two happenings), I find myself doing one of three things: either I walk briskly for physical exercise, or I lie down and rest, or I sink into a spontaneous meditation. I have no

preference. When I begin the walk or lie down on the bed, japa (Om Namah Shivaya) begins spontaneously. It really does not seem to matter, one way or the other, whether the interval is five minutes or thirty minutes.

3. While I go through the motions of daily routine in life, there is a very distinct feeling deeper down of an eternal Presence against the background of which life flows in the daily routine, including the natural, biological, spontaneous reactions in the body-mind organism.

4. I have found myself gradually avoiding unnecessary journeys and even unnecessary action — both physical and mental — and preferring to stay put. Also, gradually, small talk and social gossip ceased to interest me: I read less and less of fiction, and finally ceased reading it altogether. Winning an argument no longer seems relevant or important. And, most interestingly, day dreaming and conceptualizing about odd matters just never seems to happen. If daily living offers something to witness, witnessing happens; otherwise, I seem to sit or lie down or walk about in a state of what I would call non-witnessing, when the mind is all but totally silent, and there is nothing to witness.

5. While I find myself continuing to observe certain disciplines that have become a matter of routine habit — for example, meditation and reciting certain traditional *stotras* — it is noticed very clearly that these disciplines are no longer a source of stress inasmuch as it seems not to matter at all if circumstances sometimes interrupt the routine. What used to be once a matter of compulsion now seems part of the

daily happening, which is merely witnessed as such.

6.   It is clearly noticed that the pleasure that has occurred in the moment is thoroughly enjoyed to the full — and shared with others whenever possible, and that such pleasure does not at any time give rise to any fear of the pain that the next moment might bring. It is also realized, more and more, that the pain of the moment can be a source of immense pleasure through the relief that happens when the pain ceases. One sometimes wonders if the negative pleasure of the relief from pain is not fully as acceptable as any positive pleasure!

7.   It is very clearly noticed that the acceptance of duality as the very basis of the phenomenal manifestations and its functioning that we know as 'life' and 'daily living' — has become so very deep that the judgment of someone being good or bad, efficient or inefficient, responsible or irresponsible, hardly ever arises. Even when it sometimes does arise, it is clearly seen as the spontaneous, natural, biological reaction in the body-mind instrument, and not one's own personal reaction.

8.   The understanding that it is the same noumenal Source that has become the phenomenal manifestation has become so deeply embedded in one's being, that no conceptualizing ever takes place about the 'Source.' Thinking about the unthinkable does not happen.

9.   The total, unqualified acceptance of non-doership has resulted in the total cessation of all conceptualizing about

terms like attachment and detachment, renunciation and acceptance.

10. The occasional, sudden realization that the absence of conceptualizing and objectivizing is itself the natural state of the eternal Presence, brings about an emotion of utter humility and deepest gratitude in that moment.

11. An enormous sense of compassion arises for the common spiritual seeker who goes through great frustration after years of self-discipline (sadhana), with "weariness to the body", "fatigue to the tongue", and "distress to the mind", as Janaka says in the *Ashtavakra* Gita. He does not seem to see or realize what now seems to me to be an obvious fact: all that we could ever possibly BE must inevitably be the Source (or Consciousness or Primal Energy), which is *all there* is; and what we *appear to be* cannot be anything but a phenomenal object, through each of which the Primal Energy functions.

12. With the realization that living in essence is merely the response of each sense when in contact with its respective object, without any real volition, *there is an actual experience* that I do not really live my life but that life is being lived through me, as much as it is lived through every body-mind organism.

13. With the experience of life being lived by itself through the billions of body-mind organisms, all speculation about bondage and liberation seems as utterly superfluous and meaningless as the speculation about birth and death.

14. With the experience of life being lived by itself, it seems amazing how easily each problem seems to resolve itself, allowing each dilemma to arrive spontaneously at its natural solution. 'Me' and 'other' actually turn out to be just different perceptions.

15. I seem to have really seen the beauty of money only when I had sufficient money to give away a decent part of it, and realized that the true fulfillment can only come from giving.

16. With the total acceptance of non-doership — everything is a happening, and not the doing by anybody — it has actually been my experience that I no longer look at the other person as a potential danger and, if I am hurt, it can only be because it was my destiny-according to the Cosmic Law — to be hurt, and that the 'other' (who ever it is) was merely the instrument through which it had to happen.

17. When my wife was in the hospital, critically ill, the certainity happened with an astonishing impact of something I had always known but not really deeply appreciated: each one of us comes into the world and leaves it precisely at the appointed time. 'Life' somehow, does not now seem all that, precious'.

18. Some time ago, a thought occurred: "I do know that life is like a dream or a movie but in that dream, will Ramana Maharshi, who is the very epitome of the sage for me, ever come to me in a personal experience?" Almost immediately, this was followed by another thought: 'Who cares?" It was quite amusing.

19. When a visitor very kindly brings a gift, if it is Scotch whisky, I keep it for my guests; if it is cheese or chocolates, it goes in the fridge; if it is anything else, the thought immediately arises: "Whom shall I pass it on to? Who would really appreciate it?"

20. My wife and I have had a lovely marriage — over sixty years — and there is a reason. Many years ago we decided that my wife would do what she liked and I would do what *she* liked! This is a joke, but in actual fact, we have noticed that each of us seems to be doing almost naturally, what the other would have chosen to do.

21. Quite some time ago, a sudden thought hit me with great impact: it is downright stupid for anyone to try to appear wiser than he is, or more handsome than he is, or better in any sense than he really is. No one is perfect in this world; acceptance is so much easier than hypocrisy, being natural so much easier than pretension.

22. Talking about non-doership with a visitor, I come to the focus of non-doership: your question is, "What do I have *to do* so that my intellectual comprehension that no one is a doer could be absolutely total and unequivocal?" The visitor agrees vehemently that that is precisely the problem. I repeat the question, sometimes twice, and then the inherent humor of the situation is suddenly realized. It has often reminded me of the quotation from Chuang-Tzu: "Where can I find a man who has forgotten words? I'd like to have a word with him."

23. I am sometimes asked: "Ramesh, how is it that at eighty-six

years of age, you seem to have the energy, enthusiasm, and freshness of a child?" When I have realized the sincerity in the question, my answer has been: "Perhaps it is because I have been lucky enough to be able to accept life as it happens and, therefore, not to go against the flow of life'

24. I remember a particular time, when I was very angry with myself because I seemed not to be able to live without moods. Then the thought occurred, *with a deep impact* that ecstasy and anger, rashness and stubbornness, modesty and arrogance arise from nowhere, from the void; I have nothing to do with them — let them be; it is the way things are; it is the way life flows. I felt, I remember, thoroughly shaken but there was great *peace,* and the understanding that this peace, this emptiness can only happen spontaneously.

25. What have I understood from a fairly long life? That life itself is uncertain, that events have a way of sorting themselves out — sometimes acceptable, sometimes not, that astonishingly often, giving leads to receiving and humility leads to glory, and that what one finally wants is harmonious stillness.

26. At some time it was noticed that while the pleasure of the moment was certainly thoroughly enjoyed, there did not arise any thought about the possibility of the lack of that pleasure; that the social and financial position of the moment was accepted without any comparison with others; that the authority in any field was exercised with a natural smoothness, without any thought of criticism or competition

from others; that physical health in the moment, without fear of future illness, was recognized with gratitude; that virtue as such is a natural happening and not a personal achievement.

27.   It is been clearly noticed that as the activities proceed during the day, with all their usual problems and dilemmas, there does not exist at all any physical strain or mental stress. There seems to be a constant awareness of repose and relaxation.

28.   It is very clearly noticed that whatever happens in daily living, while one certainly participated in all the events actively, one really does not care whether an event continues or stops suddenly, whether or not there would be more or less of it in the future. Finally, one truly does not care at all if the body should fall down dead the next minute.

29.   I have found myself reluctant to give suggestions or advice unless it is specifically asked for. Even then I do not expect it to be accepted.

30.   So, how do I live my daily life? The answer, I find, is: "Having already done in each past moment whatever needed to be done about the future, I now live in the present moment, without bothering to think about the future."

31.   What about personal duty and responsibility? This is the real joker in the pack. With the total acceptance that nothing can happen unless it is the Will of God, according to a Cosmic Law, the question of personal duty and

responsibility is as irrelevant as legs on a snake.

32.   Finally, in actual daily living, what is the feeling I have about what I am? In order to ask a question or give an answer, there has to be Consciousness. And in phenomenality there must necessarily be a three-dimensional object in the manifestation. Consequently, in the functioning of the manifestation — life as we know it — the constant feeling in me is that l am Consciousness functioning through the object as a separate entity. Therefore, I cannot commit a sin, I cannot commit a mistake. Everything is precisely what is supposed to be, the way it is.

Ramesh S. Balsekar
ॐ

Dear God,

This is my letter of eternal gratitude to You.

You gave me birth in a most respected Hindu family, but not high enough in social status to make me proud.

You gave me a physical form well-admired for its perfection, but it was small enough to keep me humble.

You gave me education high enough to be most useful in life, but not high enough to make me proud.

You gave me a career in which You took me high enough to be admired, but not high enough to make me arrogant.

You gave me a wife and family, for which I have always been eternally grateful, but You did not spare me some grief to remind me not to forget what life is all about, and to be always grateful for what I do have.

You did not forget to place an adequate number of temptations in my way, so that I may not be too critical of others who have to face their own temptations.

I am now 84, and perhaps the only wish that remains is that the long life You have given me will not carry a burden at the end. But in that case, I know You will also give me the necessary courage to go with it. You gave me a lot to show me how little is needed to be content, and how much could be given away.

And, undoubtedly, the most important of all — as if the bounty You have showered on me were not enough —You crowned Your achievement by using this psychosomatic apparatus to convey to the world the most important message of Advaita. Truly I am blessed. Or indeed, my Beloved, have You not blessed Yourself?

Finally, it occurs to me, if You were to design for Yourself a life in phenomenality, could it have been much different from this one?

And, for this thought, no tears are enough to wash Your Noumenal feet.

Ramesh S. Balsekar

Talks with Ramesh On March 4, 2006

on: • Effort on the spiritual path.
      • The difference of the ego of a sage and a seeker, an ordinary person.
      • The two aspects of an ego.
      • Decisions need to be made.
      • The basis of daily living.
      • Freewill.
      • I can never ever commit a sin.
      • The society is entitled to reward or punish what society considers as 'my action'.
      • How do I live my life?
      • Peace and harmony with the other, that creates peace within oneself.
      • The dog's ego, the sage's ego.
      • How to find the ego.

RAMESH   Go ahead.

VISITOR   My question is about the topic of effort.

RAMESH   Effort, yes.

V   ...effort on the spiritual path. And when I was here the other day I had a sense that a prescription for moving towards this goal of enlightenment is to understand in the deepest way possible that there is no doer.

RAMESH   Yes.

V   And so, from my perspective, that seems like effort
…. there is an intention and an effort that takes place.

RAMESH   Look, I tell you. I want to have a drink from this cup.
Do I not have to make an effort to lift that cup to my lips?

V   Yes.

RAMESH: Should I think: I have made that effort? My requirement
of needing to drink, effort gets made, Paul.

V   Right.

RAMESH   Do I have to think that 'I' have made the effort? No!
That's the problem. Effort gets made!

V   There is still a cause and effect that happens … in the
process there is first an emotional …there is the arm, there is the
drinking

RAMESH   That's it!

V   Correct.

RAMESH   And that is why I say: what is the basis of daily living?
Where effort is needed, effort gets made.

V   Ahh.

RAMESH   Where effort is needed, effort gets made... Alright, I decide: I shall not do anything today. I'll take the day off, I even won't get out of my bed. I decide it. But in any situation ... I decided, not to go out of bed ... and then You find Yourself going to the bathroom... What happened? The effort got made.

V   Sure.

RAMESH   You are hungry, you have got to eat. You shout for someone to get You some food ... 'You' have to eat it. Effort will be made to put it in your mouth.

V   But, what it comes to, turning to the spiritual path is, that...

RAMESH   Exactly the same thing happens. Exactly the same thing 'happens'! First, you think, 'You' are on the spiritual path, isn't that right?

V   It's true, yes.

RAMESH   That's in itself not right!

V   Because there is no doer.

RAMESH   No, no. You are on the spiritual path, because you are supposed to be on the spiritual path and not on the path to make money. Your Destiny, God's Will, Cosmic Law ... according to Your Destiny, God's Will, Cosmic Law the seeking has to happen through this body-mind organism and through this ego for a particular thing. In some cases it's money, in some cases fame; in a third case: power; fourth case: spirituality or being one with God.

Whatever the ego is seeking…is precisely what he is supposed to seek… according to his Destiny, God's Will, Cosmic Law. Therefore, someone who is seeking money need not feel guilty about seeking money. Someone seeking fame need not feel guilty that he is seeking fame and someone else is seeking 'God'. I am seeking money, I am seeking fame…he is seeking God, what a good fellow he is! He will go to heaven, and we will go to hell!

Tell me, didn't you have that in mind, Paul? Therefore my main point is: whatever the ego seeks, is precisely what he is supposed to seek according to his Destiny, God's Will, Cosmic Law. That's where life starts. And what is more, the body-mind organism through which money is to be sought — or fame, or God — the programming in that body-mind organism, the genes ... a powerful factor... and the conditioning will be such, that the body-mind organism will have been constructed for money to be sought, or power, or fame to be sought, or God to be sought. We don't give enough credit to Nature. If God wanted seeking God, spiritual seeking, to happen, or, money, or, fame… so the body-mind organism is usually created so that that kind of seeking will happen… and therefore the effort will naturally get made towards that object.

V   Right. And in my thinking, I think at a certain point that effort becomes useless, because effort comes from the ego and the ego can't ... I am used in thinking in terms of: if the ego is being removed, okay, to become...

RAMESH   Ego being removed is one of the worst misconceptions that can happen.

V   Right, right. However it is…

RAMESH   One of the worst confusions any spiritual seeker can have is to aim for the ego to be removed.

V   Right.

RAMESH   You have no idea… or perhaps you do… what tremendous frustration that can cause!

V   Well, it seems impossible for the ego to remove itself; no, for one thing…

RAMESH   Would you expect the ego to commit *hara-kiri*, to commit suicide? Which ego will commit suicide? Therefore, one of the most important things… for the spiritual seeker to understand is — whether he seeks money, fame or power — until the last breath the seeker 'Paul' will be the ego.

It is the ego who starts the seeking and who decides whether he has got what he is seeking or has not got what he is seeking.

Therefore, the core-question for a spiritual seeker is — truly that is from my perspective the most important — the sage responds to his name being called, therefore there is an ego which makes the sage a separate entity, a separate entity who responds to his name being called.

The sage responds to his name being called, therefore there is a separate entity who has responded to the call from a separate entity. The ordinary person also responds to his name being called, therefore the ego of the sage is precisely like the ego of the ordinary person. The basis of the ego being identification with a particular body-mind organism with a name as a separate entity, which is exactly the same, whether it is a sage or an ordinary person. Therefore, in fact, the ego of the ordinary person was the one who was seeking God or Enlightenment. And it is the ego of the ordinary person — with the Understanding that he has — the ego has become a sage.

V   Right. So, you say, there is an ego up till his very last breath.

RAMESH   So, what is the core question? Paul, what is the core question?

V   Well, I am... I am sorry for interrupting you, please.

RAMESH   The core-question is, the sage has to have an ego, the ordinary person has to have an ego, therefore: what is the difference between the ego of the sage and the ego of the seeker, or ordinary person? That is the core question. Not that the sage has given up the ego, he can't. That is the core question: what is the difference between the ego of the sage and the seeker, or an ordinary person? That is the core question!
          And the answer is extraordinarily simple. In the ego of the sage it has so "happened" that the sense of personal doership has been totally removed.
          In a body a certain part can be removed and yet, in most cases, the man will still live... without that particular physical part. In the case of an ego — what is the ego, basically identification with a particular body-mind organism and a particular name as a separate entity — what is removed, what gets removed? In the ego of a sage it is the sense of personal doership. That, for me, is

the only difference between the seeker, a seeker who is still seeking, and a seeker where the ego stops seeking, that becomes a sage. That is the only thing, total apperception that no one can possibly be the doer in this world, the total apperception: thinking happens, doing happens, experiencing happens but, there is no individual 'doing', the thinking, or doing the doing, or doing the experiencing. That is as simple as that.

In other words, the ego has two aspects. The physical aspect is identification with a particular name and form as a separate entity. That is the basis of the ego... with or without the sense of personal doership.

The ego of the animal is only the first part. The ego of an animal is only identification with a particular name and form as a separate entity. Your pet dog is a separate entity. He doesn't want another dog to come near him when he eats his food, he wouldn't like his master Paul to be friendly with any other dog. Separate entity! But in the animal there is no sense of personal doership.

Therefore, in the case of your pet dog, Paul, you give him enough food to eat, you keep him clean, take him for a walk when he wants, and let him sit in your lap when you are reading your paper ... honestly, the dog wants nothing more, that is the perfect life for it. Why? Because he doesn't have a sense of personal doer ship and the thinking mind.

The human being is unhappy, mainly because he has mind, mind-intellect, which makes him want and think of them, and makes the sense of doership: what shall I do, to get what I want? That is the difference between the man and the animal, and that is why the animal is quite happy and the human being is not. That is the only difference: the sense of personal doership.

The sense of personal doership, Paul, is so strong, that

you believe: without the sense of personal doership, how can I live? How can I live? The point is, even without the sense of personal doership a part of the Understanding is: even without the sense of personal doership most of the doing gets done - most of the doing happens.

What is the very basis of daily living? The basis of daily living is, whether for Paul and me now, or for a caveman five thousand years ago, or anyone in future... for any human being at any time, at any place, daily living has to be the same: the human being has to deal with the situation in which he finds himself... that is the essence of daily living.

And what is 'dealing with a situation'? Dealing with a situation means: 'I' decide what I want in that situation and 'I' decide to do whatever I want. It is totally my decision what I shall do to get what I want, and I do it!

For instance, in a situation I may decide: now has finally come a situation, in which there is a very good chance of my getting something for which I have waited for a long time. But I decide I shall not do anything illegal or immoral. No one forces me... I decide it, it's my own free will. Whereas in an identical situation the psychopath would say: I don't care a damn. I will do whatever is necessary, including murder. If there is a problem later I shall deal with it. And that's what I do, and that's what the psychopath does. And that truly is the only daily living as far as the individual doer is concerned. After that, what happens? After that — and that is everybody's experience, mine and that of the psychopath — actually what happens has never ever been in anyone's control.

So, what do these two facts of life tell us? These two facts of life tell us: the human being has to have total 'free will' for daily living to happen. But everybody's lifetime experience is that

that *free will is worthless in practice*. The most important conclusion I have come to is, the human being has to have free will for life to happen, but everybody's experience is that the free will of human being is worthless in practice. And even a little introspection will make clear to the human being that, even in theory, his free will is worthless.

Even in theory his free will is based only on two factors, his genes and his conditioning. Conditioning is what happens every moment from moment... to moment, whatever I read, whatever I listen to, whatever I experience, everything all the time is amending or changing my conditioning. So, at any moment, whatever I think as my free will is based entirely on these two factors, my genes and my up-to-date conditioning, which God made; I have no control over either my genes or my conditioning. Therefore in theory my free will is worthless because I have to accept whatever God makes.

So, conclusion: I do have certainly free will, because without free will I cannot function, but both, in theory and practice, my 'free will' is worthless. In theory my free will is based on two factors — genes and conditioning — which God made. Therefore, whatever I have just done, whatever I have done all my life, is exactly what God expected me to do at each time.

Therefore, it is very clear to me: I can never, ever, commit a sin!.. whatever the 'sin', whatever the concept of sin, if I think sin is something that God did not expect me to do. And yet, there is nothing I can do which God would not expect. Therefore in theory I don't have to fear God because I cannot commit a 'sin'. I don't have to fear God at any time. In other words, the understanding clearly is, it is God acting through me ... and whatever it is, that God expects to produce through me, God has created the genes and the conditioning in this body-mind instrument, you see. Therefore I do not have to fear God; and if I do not have to fear God, nothing stops me from loving God, my creator. One cannot be God-fearing and God-loving at the same time.

But the fact remains: I cannot commit a sin, I do not have to fear any punishment from God... but, I still have to live my life in society.

I don't have to fear God for any punishment, but I do have to fear the society for the punishment the society is entitled to give me. If the society considers what has 'happened'... *one* of three things... what is my experience? Sometimes I got what I wanted, sometimes I have not got what I wanted and sometimes what I got was beyond my expectation. And the society considers what has 'happened' as my action. Situation after situation, I do whatever I like. One of three things has happened; the society has considered that as my action, judged that as good or bad, rewarded me or punished me. Reward from society has meant pleasure, punishment from society has meant pain... and that has been life over any numbers of years. Life has meant for everyone: one moment pleasure, another moment pain... and no one could know what the next moment will bring.

V   Everything is preordained.

RAMESH   Everything is predetermined, preordained.

V   When I was young, when I was thirteen, I was obsessed wanting to understand the meaning of life.

RAMESH   Now, doesn't that tell you, that 'you' were not obsessed? You were supposed to be obsessed.

V   Well, it happened.

RAMESH   There it is! How can a thirteen year old boy obsess himself? A thirteen year old boy can only 'be' obsessed.

V   Okay, yeah, well, that's what happened. When fifteen I had, I guess, what you might call a free sample of experience.

RAMESH   Yes.

V   Which was quite profound and I didn't understand it.

RAMESH   What did happen?

V   Well, I invented a series of little exercises that were similar to meditation. And I was doing those exercises when I slipped into a state where...

RAMESH   At fifteen?

V   At fifteen. I had been doing those for one year or one and a half years. I slipped into a state where it seemed like all the boundaries, which separated me from everything else, disappeared and there was a sense of peace where I was at the edge of a very large lake where I have been many times and there was a sense of: even there was a hurricane to wipe everything out, it wouldn't matter, it wouldn't affect this state of peace that was so deep and profound. There was no thinking, except occasionally thoughts would arise almost as if they were in a bubble, okay. And one of the thoughts that arose was upon seeing an aeroplane flying overhead and there was an awareness that ... normally I would have been annoyed at the noise and intrusion into my space, but at that moment there was the realization that ... a complete knowing ... that it was perfect, exactly perfect the way it was. Everything in the environment was exactly perfect. And at a certain point I got up, walking through the camp around where my family was camping and I encountered two other teenagers that I didn't know, well, one that I knew and the other that I did not know, and he introduced me to his female friend and I found that I couldn't carry on a conversation but the love that I felt was so overwhelming, it was uncontainable, and I just looked at him and said: I know this will sound strange to you, but I tell you, I love you both. And it was so powerful and they stood there and just looked at me... I stood there and looked at them, and there was this feeling. And I was not intending to say: I love you both, I never did before.

RAMESH   Paul, in other words, you were not embarrassed that you told them that you love them both.

V   Oh, no, no, no. There was...

RAMESH   Would anybody dare to tell them: I love you both? Obviously *they* were embarrassed.

V   I stood there a few moments then walked away and a thought appeared: I wonder if this is how Jesus felt two thousand years ago. And, so anyway, I spend the next few hours in this state, went to sleep and woke up in the morning with the thought: holy shit, what was that? you know. I was scared.

RAMESH   You were back to normal, back to normal.

V   I was back to normal, yeah. [*Laughter*] It was, you know, the thought of: was that some psychotic event? You know, I had no idea. ....And I stopped to do these little exercises because I didn't want to have that to happen again.

RAMESH   Oh, really? You didn't want any more free samples?

V: I had no idea what it was.

RAMESH   You didn't know what it was, but it surely was pleasant.

V   Oh, it was very pleasant.

RAMESH   Then, why did you stop it? You didn't want any more free samples?

V   Well, I was on a quest to understand what truth was, what the meaning of life was. I thought it was an intellectual idea, but it was actually an experience.

RAMESH   What you thought was, what happened, was an aberration...

V   Yes.

RAMESH   ...an aberration which will keep you away from your strict goal.

V   Yes.

RAMESH   So, you said: no more aberration!

V   It scared me, I didn't know what it was. However, in retrospect, it took me some years of reading to figure out what it was. So, I know that it is an extraordinary state, it is not like any ego-state, that I've experienced.

So I stayed on the spiritual path, you know, for almost my whole life, and I tried to understand how to... it just seems to me that... first you have to reach down to pick up the cup, that there is an effort involved. And yet, at a certain point I know, that I can't make an effort to achieve that goal, because... there is always an 'I' that feels that he is making an effort that will prevent it from happening. So...

RAMESH   So long as there is a sense of personal doership.

V   Right, right. So, you know, I was here two days ago. I had the sense that your prescription for reaching that goal is to reach a deeper and deeper space of non-doership. And that will be an effort.

RAMESH   You know where you have gone wrong? What you express as my "prescription" would only be a "description"!

V   A description, okay.

RAMESH   ...what people, when we talk on it, take as a prescription. That also happened, has to happen. And when I want to talk, whether I talk, what I say is a description of what happened. But the illusion — the 'me' — has taken it as a prescription. And the 'Final Understanding' is precisely this, that it is not a prescription, it is a description.

V   You see, the ego still has to make an effort to consider it as a description.

RAMESH   The ego turns the description into a prescription. It is the ego that turns the description into a prescription. So, if you had not stopped that aberration, may be very soon the sense of personal doership would be gone. But you were not supposed to, and you didn't.

So, now the question really is: when ultimately the sense of personal doership disappears, how is it possible for that ego to live the rest of its life? How is it possible for the ego to live the rest of his life? How does an ego, with the Understanding happening, live the rest of his life?

V   There is a book by Susan Seagull, called *Collision With The Infinite*, where she gives a wonderful description, where she describes how she is at a bus stop in Paris, when the bus comes and she gets on the bus, but her awarene stays about here and she watches herself pay the fare, sit down next to a woman, having a conversation, with no sense of doership, that she describes: it just did it by itself, the body-mind just performed all these things what she watched. So it is a wonderful description.

RAMESH   Description, Paul, of what?

V   Of non-doership.

RAMESH   No, it is a description of a 'free sample', a free sample, indeed! It is a description of an experience.

V   Yes. In her case it didn't go away. And she spend the next

ten years in psychotherapy, thinking that she was crazy. [*Laughter*]
RAMESH   Therefore she did not think it was a free sample.
Therefore, if she had only thought of it as a free sample — even as
an aberration — free sample or aberration, the most important
point is, she had no control over it, nor did You have any control
over it, nor has anyone who had a 'free sample'... for a few
moments, for a few hours, for a few days, whatever it is, it is still
a free sample, a free sample which has a limited life, time-bound
... and than the ego comes back to normal. Usually what happens,
you had a free sample, and the ego likes it so much, he pursues
the free sample for more, and the more he pursues it, the farther
away the sample goes, that is, they loose it. And whatever happens
is according to their destiny.

But the point I am making is, it is only a free sample.
Don't attach too much importance to any experience! That is my
point... don't attach any importance to any free sample, however
deep, however mysterious, it is still time-bound. So, therefore my
question is: when the final understanding has happened, the free
sample has turned out to be the whole food.

Therefore when the final Understanding has happened
and the total acceptance of non-doership, how does the ego live
his life? In the *Bhagavad Gita* this question is asked and in a
number of verses, giving detailed description how a jnani or a
sage, lives. It doesn't have much relevance for you and me. It
creates a lot of confusion. One who is established in wisdom,
how does he live his life? That is the description, you see. So I
read it and said, this doesn't tell me anything.

So, if I want to tell others, what would I say? And I
started *making* notes and ultimately I came to about thirty-two
points. You have got that in the book: *How Do I Live My Life?*
That is the search because people asked: what do you do in this

second, what do you do in that second? So I wrote down all that I could think of, in deep and in detail but, in general I found it so simple. How do I live my life? Interesting, isn't it? How do I live my life? The details are in that booklet.

V   Yes.

RAMESH   In practice you have no idea how easy it is, how simple and easy it is. What is daily living, Paul, for me or you?

V   So, will you describe it later?

RAMEH   Therefore, based on that, in any situation I do whatever I feel like doing, knowing that both, in theory and practice, I have no free will. What does that mean? It means: in any situation I do whatever I feel, *as if I have free will*. I know, in theory and practice, I don't have free will but I do live my life dealing with every situation as if I have free will.

        Can anything be simpler than that? My grandson is now twenty four. He was a born actor. When he was ten he was with a troupe of fifteen to twenty actors and he was playing the role of a prince with his widowed mother.Once what happened was that on one occasion the mother forgot her lines. So what does this ten year old prince do? On the stage he sees — the play was going on — the ten years old born actor repeats her lines and then adds, isn't that so, mother? In fact, a born actor, acting not only when he is sure that he would be admired, a born actor wanting to be the whole play to be good. Teamwork... Whether it is a play or a match of cricket, anything. The real actor is a team-worker, his own success comes later. So I asked him once: what happens when you play acting? He didn't seem surprised — a ten

69

year old boy, his name is Ameya — he said, on the stage I forget that I am Ameya, I am the prince. In other words, I act as if I am the prince. It's quite interesting: I act as if I am the prince.

So, in any given situation I do whatever I feel like doing, knowing that I have no free will. I do whatever I feel as if I have free will.

I repeat, can anything be simpler than that? The actor plays the role of a prince. Put it the other way around: the beggar plays the role of a prince but on the stage he forgets that he is only a pauper; on the stage he a prince.

So, how do I live my life? Extraordinarily simple: in any situation I do whatever I have do to as if I have free will, thinking consistently in this situation: what is the best thing to do, and come to my own decision. I do whatever I feel I should do as if I have total free will. But having done it, having done it I know with equal certainty, whatever consideration I might have given to the thought, to the decision, what actually happens has never ever been in my control. My lifetime experience!

I know, in any given situation I do whatever I feel like, doing as if I have total free will giving it all due consideration but, once I have done it, after that, I merely witness whatever happens. I witness whatever happens without blaming anybody, judging anybody or condemning anybody or anything. Isn't that simple?

So I said, when I thought of if, all that long chain of verses in the *Bhagavad Gita*, I don't need them. All they mean is this, and most important, it happened so, it 'happened'!

I repeat, in any situation I give it a total thought, and finally having done whatever I have done, after that, my job is done! After that I can only witness whatever is happening as something which has to happen precisely as it is to happen according to God's Will, Cosmic Law. Therefore it's stupid to judge anything or anybody. So I accept whatever is happening, merely witness whatever is happening, I witness whatever is happening as something which has to be exactly the way it is, precisely the way it is; therefore there is no question of my judging anybody or condemning anybody, neither myself nor the other ... that is the important part, no judging — or blaming, or condemning — anybody, neither myself nor the other! Therefore there is no question of hating anybody, neither me nor the other.

So, the result of this is: total absence of hatred. I am not saying I am full of 'love'. I am taking the negative attitude: total absence of hatred either for myself or for the other. And the absence of hatred means the presence of peace and harmony. And that according to me, honestly, is all that anybody — like us, reasonably comfortable in life — can ultimately want in life: peace and harmony; harmony with the other, that creates peace with oneself.

So, what are you doing now, Paul? What part of the world are you from?

V   I live in the States.

RAMESH   United States. What are you doing, what is your business or your profession?

V   I repair chimneys.

RAMESH   I see, yes, you told me, yes. And that gives you sufficient money for your reasonable needs?

V   Yes, I live very modestly.

RAMESH   Yes, that's the point.

V   And I come to India. every winter for about three months.

RAMESH   So you have enough money to do that.

V   Yeah, yeah.

RAMESH   And therefore, according to me, Paul, you are the really wealthy man all... your wants are fulfilled. Do you create new ones? Which is what 'Pauls' normally do, Paul [*Laughter*]. Once you start to create new ones, there is no limit to it.

V   My basic needs are covered and the things that are important to me, like coming to India, I am able to do.

RAMESH   Yes. And you have been coming to India fairly regularly?

V   Yes, that is my eighth visit in nine years. I come to see Amritanandmayee Ma... Amma... she is now on tour.

RAMESH   Did you live in her ashram?

V   I lived in her ashram during the time I have been in India, and now she is on tour through India for two months, and I am travelling on the tour.

RAMESH   With her?

V   With her, yes, with the group.

RAMESH   With the group, yes, I understand.

V   I find it really so wonderful to talk with you… and you speak English, and Amma doesn't speak English.

RAMESH   And, because I have a 'mania' for clarity! Confusion makes me angry!

V2   You were talking about the ego of a saint and a dog. What is the difference between the ego of a saint and the ego of a dog?

RAMESH   The difference between the ego of a saint and God?

V2   Of a dog.

RAMESH   The difference is, the ego of the dog makes it a separate being exactly as the ego of a saint. But in the case of a dog — because the mind-intellect is not there — there was no need for understanding the meaning of life. No need of wanting to know the truth in life.

V2   The dog did not want all this.

RAMESH   And there is no need for it... but, in the case of a sage he starts with the need for it! In other words, the dog's ego is identification with a name and form as a separate entity plus ignorance.
        The sage's ego is a separate entity with total 'Understanding'. Ignorance without wanting any ignorance to be removed — in the case of a sage he starts with a separate entity with ignorance and with mind wanting, mind wanting ignorance to be removed... and that has been removed. So the ignorance of

the dog has been replaced with full Understanding of the sage. Therefore the dog: separate entity plus ignorance, the sage: separate entity plus total Understanding.

V3   This time I find myself laughing the whole time.

RAMESH   That's the whole point... the whole search is so stupid! [*Laughter*] No wonder that you are laughing the whole time.

V3   [*Laughter*]. . . and sometimes I feel embarrassed that ... You know, I look at people's faces and they turn to me, and 'huuuuh' [*Laughter*] and I can't help myself laughing. And one thing that we talked about, the ego...

RAMESH   You know what bothers many people?

V   No.

RAMESH   They see... what is your name?

V3   Ingar.

RAMESH   Ingar, of course. They see Ingar laughing with tears in her eyes [*Laughter*]. That baffles them.

V3   One of the things that may be puzzled me today was, you know, the idea that we have to kill the ego, because this is what we've been told.

RAMESH   That is a horrible misconception.

V3   Yes, I know, and there was this certain thought in my mind in saying, okay, in order to kill the ego, you first have to find it, and where is it?

RAMESH   No, that is not difficult, Ingar.

V3   No? [*Laughter*]

RAMESH   Who is the ego? The ego is the one who feels guilty about certain action she has done.

V3   Yes, okay.

RAMESH   The ego is the one who feels proud about some achievement.

V3   Yes, but you say, if you go searching for it ... if I said: where is the ego in me? I can't find it , you know, where is it?

RAMESH   Then this is the answer: who is proud, who is proud of the achievement? Who feels guilty about it, who hates someone else for hurting it? That is the ego!

V3   Yes.